READABOUT

Time and Clocks

© 1992 Franklin Watts

Franklin Watts
96 Leonard Street
London EC2A 4RH

Franklin Watts Australia
14 Mars Road
Lane Cove
NSW 2066

UK ISBN: 0 7496 0785 8

A CIP catalogue record for this book
is available from the British Library

Editor: Ambreen Husain
Design: K and Co

Printed in Hong Kong

The Publisher and Photographer
would like to thank
R. Salsbury & Sons Ltd of Guildford
for the loan of clocks and watches.

Additional photographs:
ZEFA p27

READABOUT

Time and Clocks

Text: Henry Pluckrose
Photography: Chris Fairclough

Franklin Watts
London/New York/Sydney/Toronto

What time do you get up each day?

What time do you eat lunch?
What time do you have supper?
What time do you go to bed?

There was a time
when you were a baby.
Can you remember
being very small?

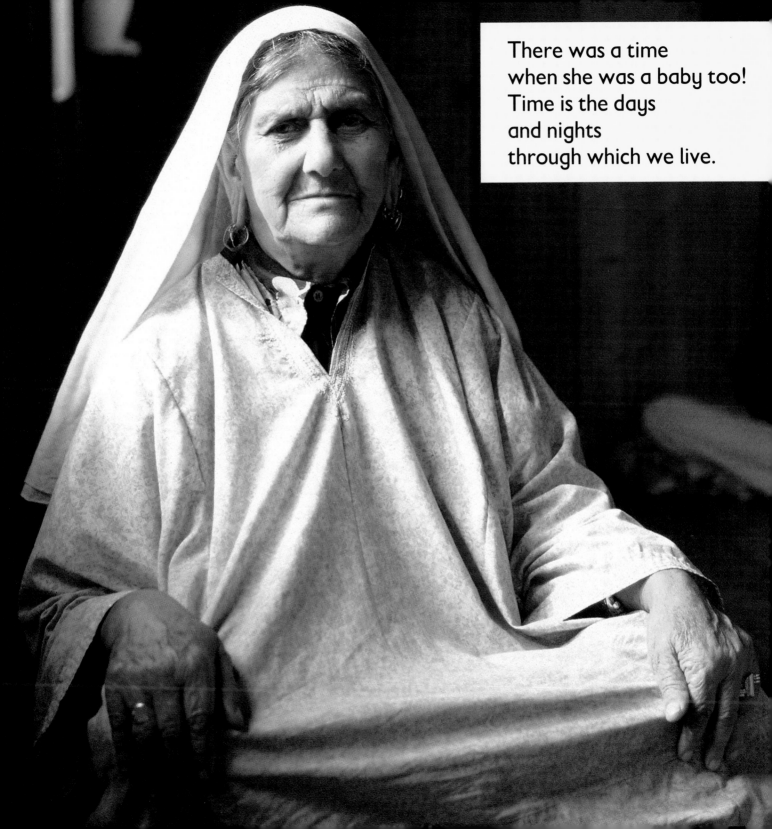

There was a time
when she was a baby too!
Time is the days
and nights
through which we live.

We can measure time in days...
daytime when it is light

and night-time when it is dark.
But sometimes we need to
measure time
more accurately than this.

Long ago people measured time
with a sundial.
The shadow marked the hour.
Can you use a sundial
on a cloudy day?

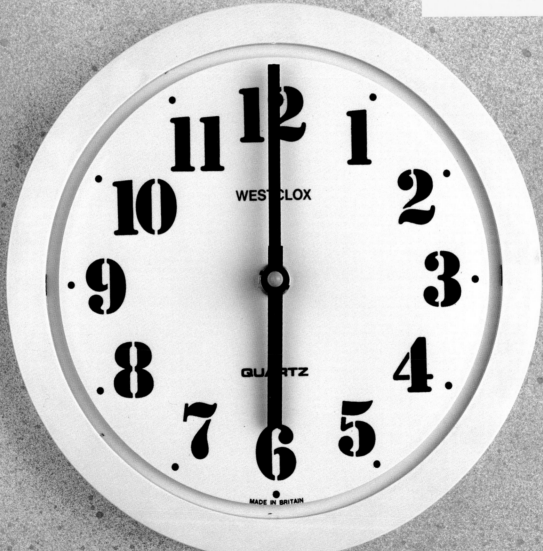

A clock can measure the passing of time more accurately than a moving shadow.

This clock has a face
and three hands.
The thin hand is called
the second hand.
It takes 60 seconds
for the second hand
to go round the clock face.
The long hand is called
the minute hand.
It takes 60 minutes
for the minute hand
to go round the clock face.

The short hand is called
the hour hand.
It takes one hour
for the hour hand
to move from one number
to the next.
It takes 12 hours
for the hour hand
to go right round
the clock face.

Have you ever looked inside a clock?
Some clocks are driven by a spring.
The spring is wound up with a key.
Some clocks are driven by a battery.

You can see clocks
in many places…
on towers,
over shops
and in stations.
These are all public clocks.

We have clocks in our houses.
This is a pendulum clock.
The pendulum swings from
side to side.
The swinging pendulum
drives the hands.

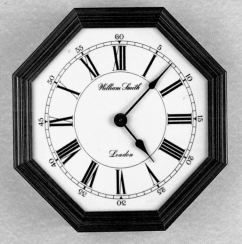

Where might you find clocks like these?

We are not always
near a clock when we need
to know the time.
We could carry a
clock with us...

but it's much easier
to use a watch.

There are many kinds of watch…
wrist watches,
watches for nurses,

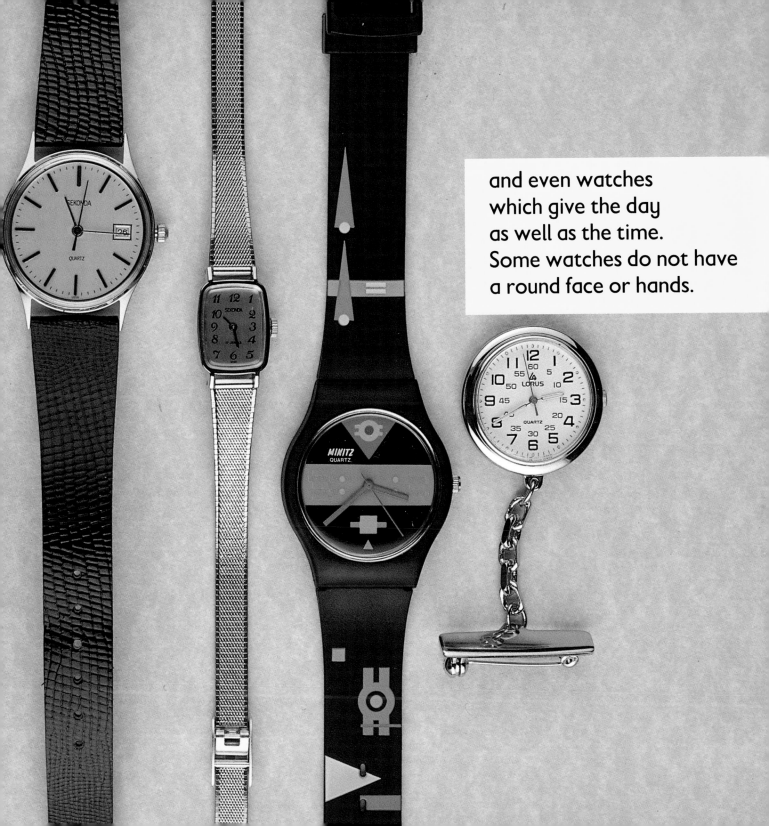

and even watches
which give the day
as well as the time.
Some watches do not have
a round face or hands.

Sometimes we need to measure
very short moments of time.
A race can be timed
with a stop watch.
The watch is started at
the beginning of the race
and is stopped
at the end.

We measure long periods
of time in days,
weeks, months and
years.

Why do we need to measure time? We need to know how long to cook food.

If we do not
measure the time correctly
the food will be spoiled.

When we go to catch a train
we need to know
what time it will leave
the station.

FLUG FLIGHT	NACH TO	ÜBER VIA	PLANM. SCHED.
BA3118	BERLIN		11 30
LH 729	FRANKFURT		11 40
LH 362	BELGRAD	MUENCHEN	11 45
SN 756	BRUESSEL		11 45
LH 174	BARCELONA		12 05
SK 626	KOPENHAGEN		12 10
BA 749	LONDON		12 15
HN 424	AMSTERDAM		12 30
LH 316	ATHEN	MUENCHEN	12 40
LH 024	OSLO	HAMBURG	12 50
LH1005	FRANKFURT		
AF 765	PARIS		

Abflüge werden nicht ausgerufen!

When we go to catch a plane we need to know what time it will leave the airport.

Where might you find
these time keepers?

People have invented
all kinds of things
to measure time.
We are told not to
waste time.
Some people even try
to save time!

Most living things never try to measure time!

About this book

All books which are specially prepared for young children are written to meet the interest of the age group at which they are directed. This may mean presenting an idea in a humorous or unconventional way so that ideas which hitherto have been grasped somewhat hazily are given sharper focus. The books in this series aim to bring into focus some of the elements of life and living which we as adults tend to take for granted.

This book develops and explores an idea using simple text and thought-provoking photographs. The words will encourage questioning and discussion – whether they are read by adult or child. Children enjoy having information books read to them just as much as stories and poetry. The younger child may ignore the written words…pictures play an important part in learning, particularly if they encourage talk and visual discrimination.

Young children acquire much information in an incidental, almost random fashion. Indeed, they learn much just by being alive! The adult who uses books like this one needs to be sympathetic and understanding of the young child's intellectual development. It offers a particular way of looking, an approach to questioning which will result in talk, rather than "correct" one word answers.

Henry Pluckrose